# Succulent Serenity

A coloring book
by Gina Spadoni & Matthew Kracht

three trees

Special thanks to our friend Liz Duarte, a ceramicist in Seattle who allowed us to photograph her handmade pots featuring her succulents, which inspired some of the illustrations in this book. She also shared photos of her Dad's amazing succulent plants, some of which also made their way into our drawings.

We hope you like coloring these as much as we enjoyed creating them. They are printed on one side only so you may detach them from the book and display your finished works of art.

Colored pencils will work great, as will crayons, gel pens and fine tipped markers – though with pens and markers, we suggest you test them on the pages reserved for this purpose in the back of the book. If they bleed through you may want to slip an extra sheet of paper behind the page you're working on.

We hope you not only have fun with this book, but that it helps you de-stress a little, too. The act of coloring can help you get into a relaxed creative zone where time slips away and you just enjoy the moment. You might have a cup of tea or a glass of wine to further unwind.

Enjoy!

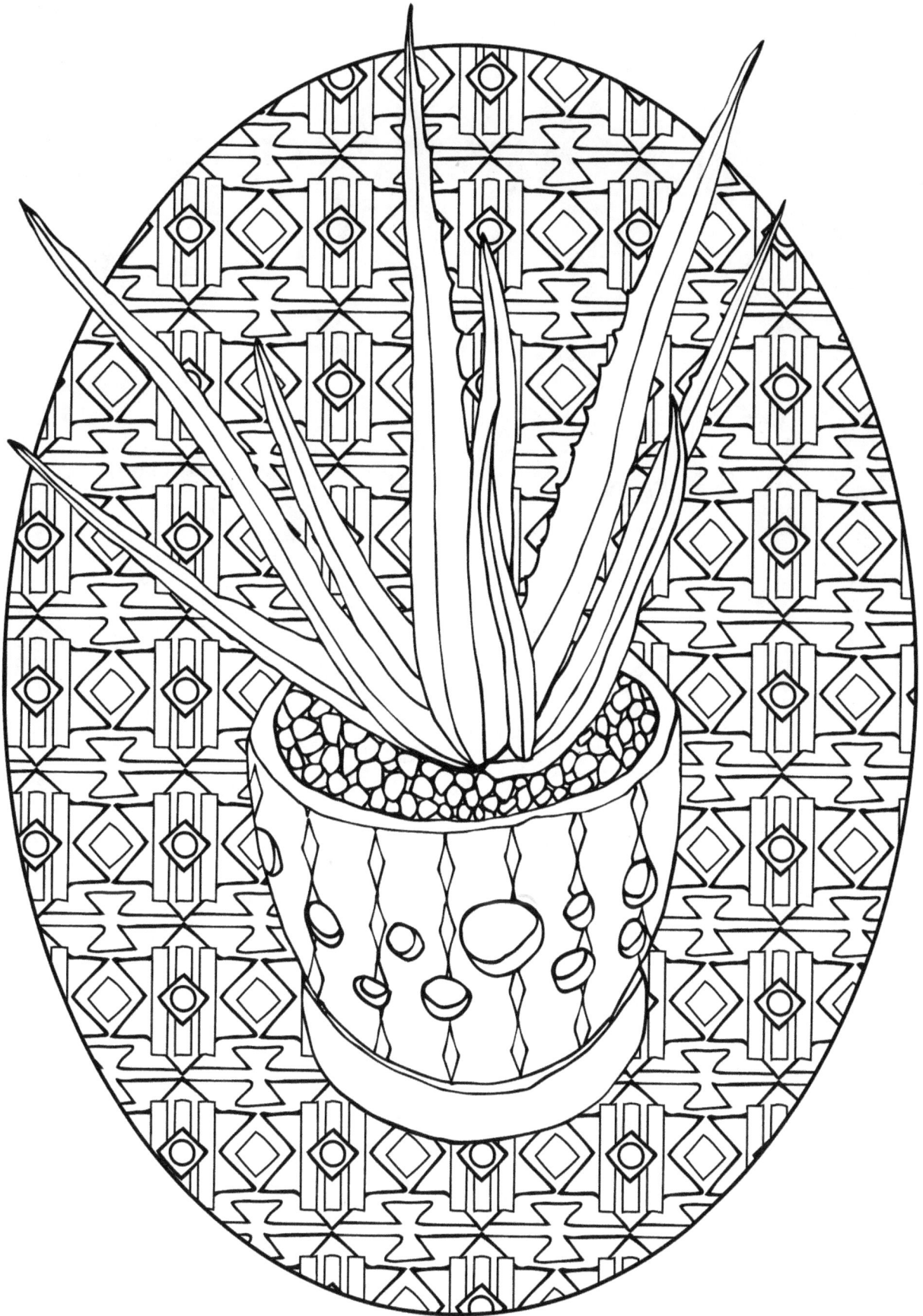

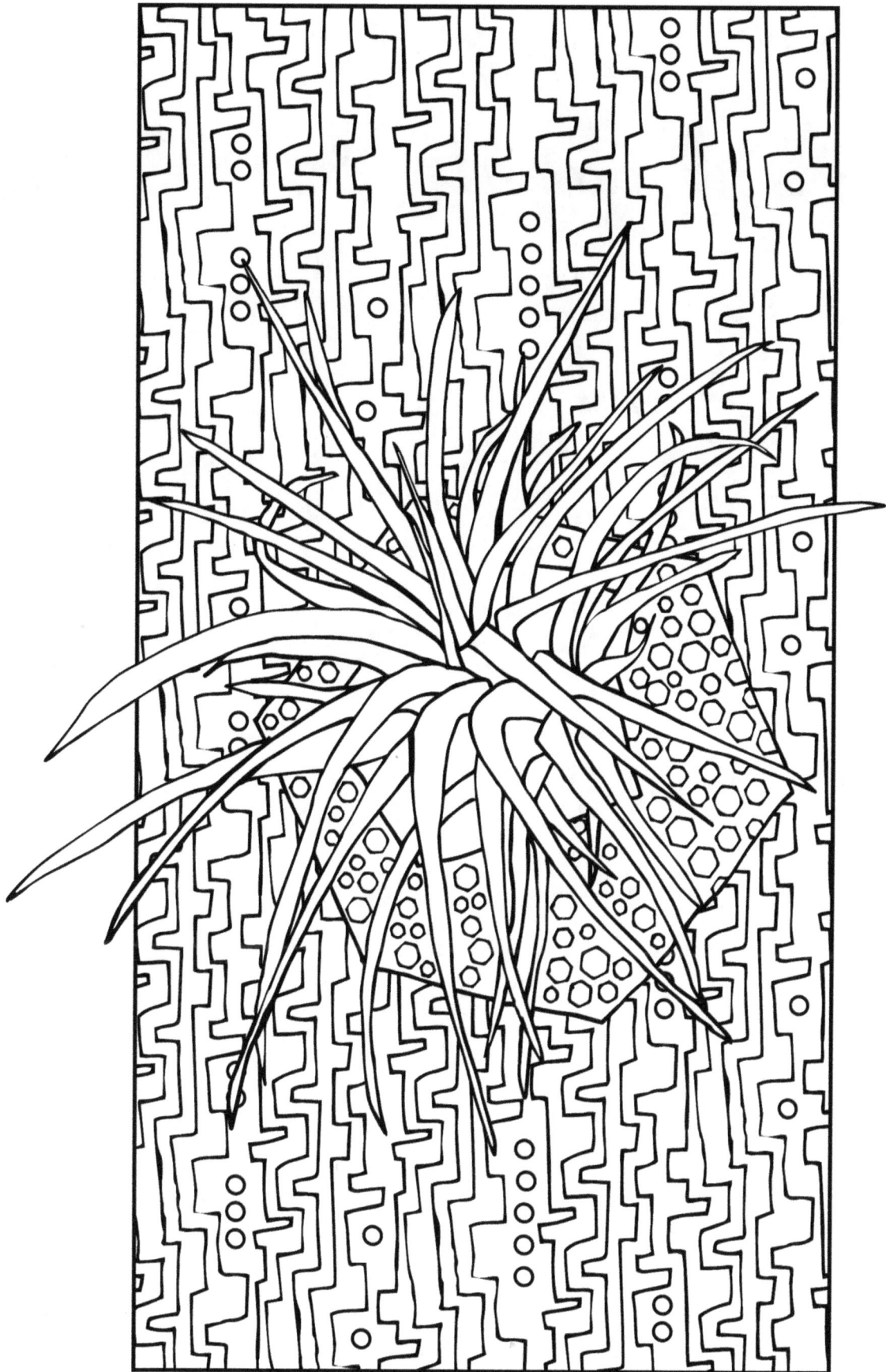

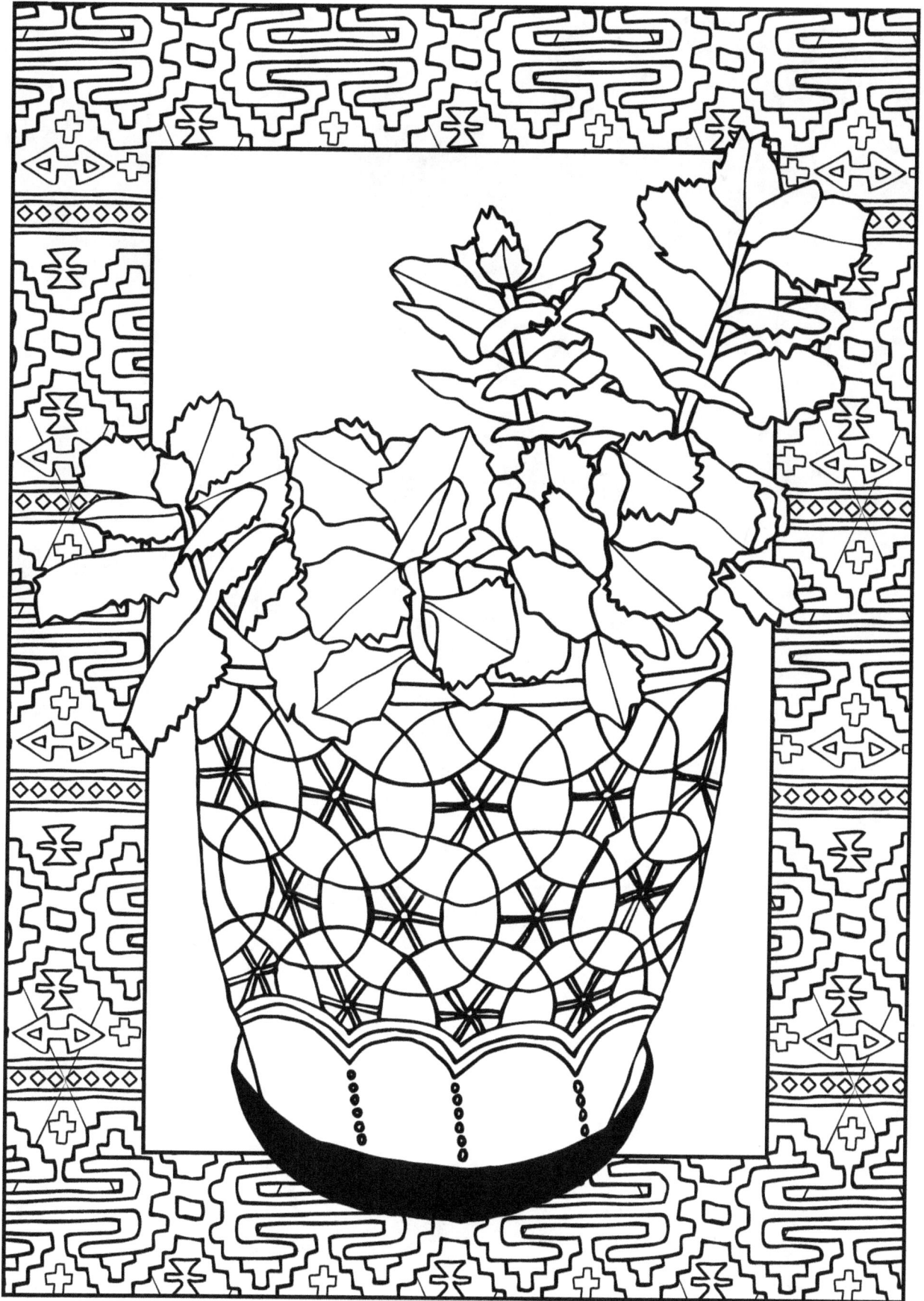

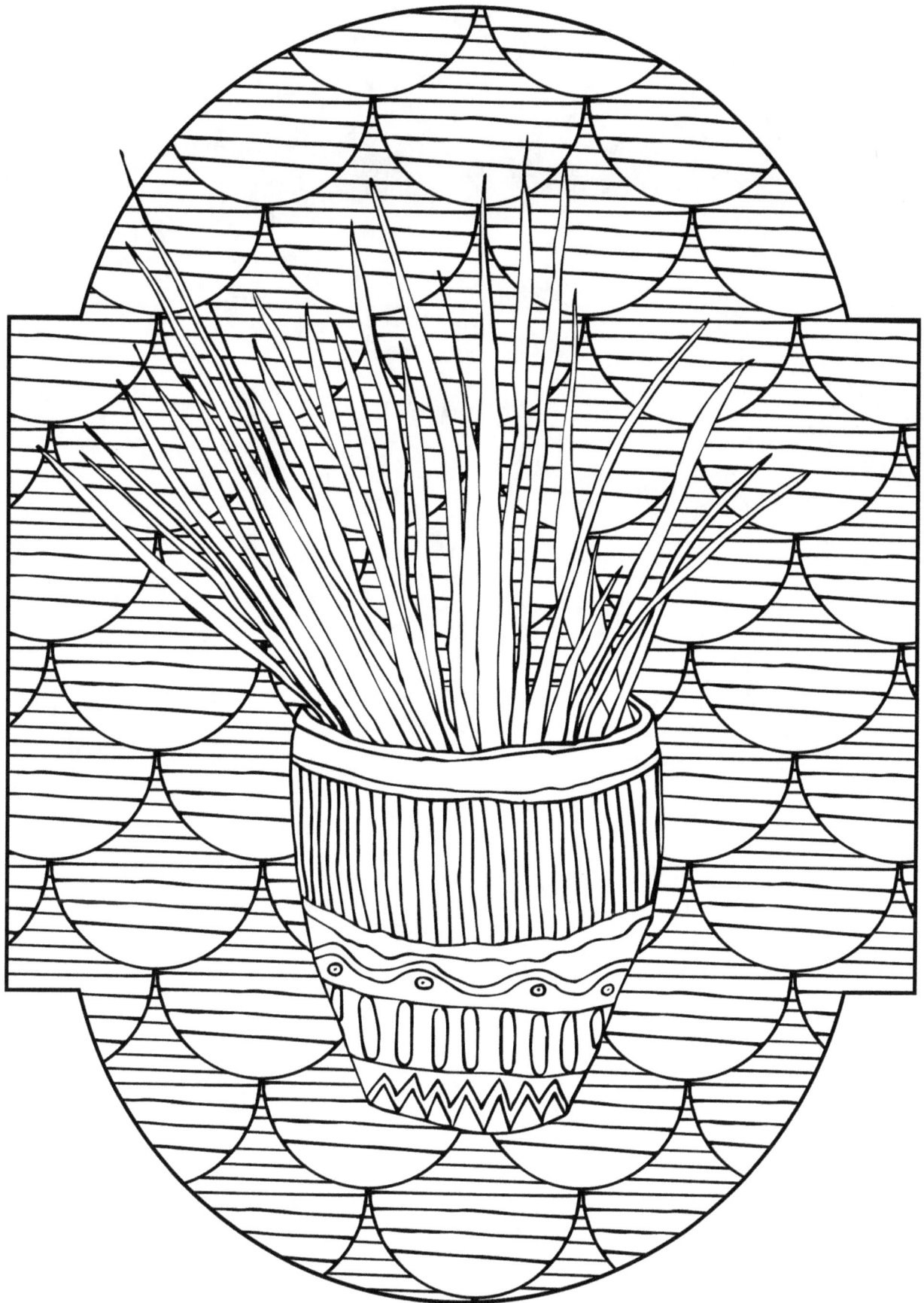

# Notes

*For testing pens & pencils, practicing new techniques, or just doodling.*

*While this paper should not bleed with most pencils, pens and markers, if you find that your ink bleeds through this page, we recommend placing a sheet of scratch-paper behind the page you're working on when coloring.*

# Notes

*For testing pens & pencils, practicing new techniques, or just doodling.*

*While this paper should not bleed with most pencils, pens and markers,
if you find that your ink bleeds through this page, we recommend placing a sheet
of scratch-paper behind the page you're working on when coloring.*

# Notes

*For testing pens & pencils, practicing new techniques, or just doodling.*

*While this paper should not bleed with most pencils, pens and markers,
if you find that your ink bleeds through this page, we recommend placing a sheet
of scratch-paper behind the page you're working on when coloring.*

## About the Authors

Gina Spadoni and Matt Kracht are a married couple who live in Seattle, Washington, and love to be creative. Gina is a writer, former librarian and competitive intelligence professional who now enjoys running an e-commerce business, practicing the art of illustration, and learning to make pottery. Matt is a professional designer by day – and a painter, photographer, and illustrator by night. When they're not engaged in some creative endeavor, Gina and Matt like to cook, hike, take walks to the beach, sample new restaurants and binge-watch television.

three trees